STEAM ON THE WAVERLEY ROUTE

STEAM
ON THE
WAVERLEY ROUTE

R. H. LESLIE

D. BRADFORD BARTON LTD

Frontispiece: Following the opening of the Settle-Carlisle line in 1876 by the Midland Railway, through trains commenced running between London (St. Pancras) and Edinburgh (Waverley), and these continued until closure of the Waverley Route in 1969. The principal daytime service was named 'The Thames-Forth Express' by the London Midland & Scottish Railway in 1927, but this lapsed with the outbreak of war in 1939 and was not reinstated. However, in the Summer of 1957 the service was given the very appropriate title of 'The Waverley', and in this view at Carlisle one of the long-serving 'A3' Pacifics from Canal shed, No.60079 *Bayardo*, backs on to the down express on 11 March 1961. [R.H. Leslie]

© copyright D. Bradford Barton   IRRC   787/25 PN   ISBN 0 85153 341 8

Printed and bound in Great Britain by R.J. Acford, Chichester, Sussex

for the publishers

D. BRADFORD BARTON LTD · Trethellan House · Truro · Cornwall · England

introduction

The main line of the former North British Railway through the border country between Edinburgh and Carlisle, known from its earliest days as the Waverley Route, was rich in character and romance, gaining much of its popularity from the dramatic scenery through which it passed, as well as from its historical associations.

Like so many other lines, its origins were of a purely local nature, the first section being the Edinburgh & Dalkeith Railway opened in 1831 to a gauge of 4'6" and operated by horse traction. In 1845 this line was acquired by the recently formed North British Railway, who by 1849 had extended the route to Galashiels and Hawick, changed the gauge to the standard 4'8½" and adopted steam haulage of its trains.

Hawick remained the terminal until, in 1859, after a continuous legal battle with its arch-rival, the Caledonian Railway, the North British at last won parliamentary approval to construct the extension to Carlisle, known as the Border Union Railway, and completed in July 1862. Even then, the Caledonian did its best to thwart the rival concern by acquiring the land to the north-east of Carlisle, thus preventing direct access to the city. However, not to be outdone, the North British bought the historic Port Carlisle Railway and obtained running powers over the Caledonian line from near Canal Junction into Citadel station.

By nature of the country through which it passed, the line was always difficult to operate. The severe southbound climb to Falahill, a mere eighteen miles from Edinburgh, and the equally long, hard gradients to Whitrope in the Cheviot Hills between Hawick and Newcastleton, were made even more difficult by the continuous, and in places severe, curvature of the line, which precluded any high-speed running. Nevertheless, the through trains between London St. Pancras and Edinburgh, inaugurated following the opening of the Midland Railway's Settle-Carlisle line in 1876 and maintained until closure of the line in 1969, provided a reasonably fast and convenient service for the inhabitants of the Border towns.

The name 'Waverley' had its origins in the works of Sir Walter Scott, who had been inspired to use the name for a character in his first novel by a visit to the ruined Cistercian monastery in Surrey at Waverley Abbey, near Farnham. Later, it became the collective title for the whole series of his novels, which found tremendous popularity with the literary public for many years.

The North British had named their splendid Edinburgh station, Waverley, and as the new line passed within about a mile of Scott's estate at Abbotsford in the beautiful country-side along the River Tweed, it seemed very appropriate to adopt the name to publicise the route. In 1877 a series of locomotives built by Drummond especially for the Edinburgh-Carlisle trains were known as the 'Abbotsford' class and named after places along the line. Indeed, the Waverley novels were to provide names for many other North British and London & North Eastern locomotives, in the years to come.

Many types of locomotives hauled the Waverley Route passenger and freight trains down the years. In later North British days, principal expresses were hauled by the majestic 'Atlantics' which, more than any other class, seemed to represent the spirit and romance of the line. By the late 1920s, the new 'A3' Pacifics were being drafted to the line to provide extra power, and in post-war days most of the LNER Pacific classes appeared regularly—even the stream-lined 'A4's which could hardly demonstrate their speed capabilities over such a sinuous line. After Nationalisation in 1948, LMS and BR Standard classes began to appear—although their use was rather limited, for the traditional North British and LNER types still bore the brunt of the work. As with most lines, certain locomotives came to be associated more than others with the day-to-day operating, and there was no more appropriate setting for the lilting, syncopated exhaust beat of the Gresley three-cylinder classes of 'A3', 'V2', 'K3' and 'D49' as they battled with the gradients through the border hills.

With one exception, the photographs in this volume were taken during the twenty years between 1946 and 1966, a period which saw the gradual withdrawal of all the older locomotives, followed by the eventual demise of steam working. Now, alas, the line too has gone for ever, so perhaps this volume will provide a lasting memory of one of Britain's fine railways—the Waverley Route.

My grateful thanks are due to the many photographers who have contributed their work to this volume, and to Rae Montgomery for producing the excellently detailed map.

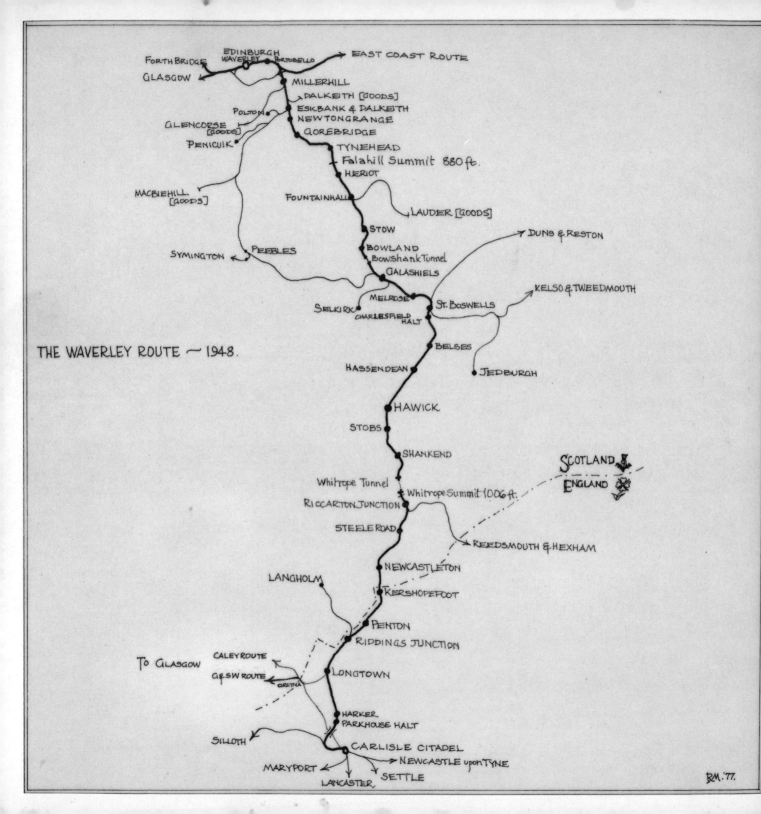

THE WAVERLEY ROUTE — 1948.

In the early 1950s, the 12.25 p.m. Saturday stopping train from Hawick to Carlisle was usually hauled by one of the former North British Railway 'D30' Class 4-4-0s from Hawick shed, although a 'D49', and very occasionally a 'D11', would appear at times. No.62435 *Norna,* in very clean condition, arrives at Carlisle on 25 January 1953. [R.H. Leslie]

Overleaf: Several of the 'D49' Class 4-4-0s ended their days working from Hawick shed and were usually employed on Hawick–Carlisle local trains. In this scene No.62712 *Morayshire,* the last survivor, arrives at Carlisle with the 12.28 p.m. from Hawick on 11 February 1961. This locomotive was later privately purchased and restored to its original condition, as an example of a Darlington-built LNER design, and is at present housed at the Scottish Railway Preservation Society depot at Falkirk.

[R.H. Leslie]

Until they began to be displaced by diesels on the East Coast main line in the early 1960s, the 'A4' Pacifics were rarely seen on Waverley Route trains. At this time their appearances were becoming rather more frequent, and by a lucky chance No.60009 *Union of South Africa* was captured hauling the down 'Waverley' away from Carlisle on 14 April 1961. The train is diverging from the Glasgow main line onto the sharply-curved spur to Canal Junction and the Waverley Route proper.

[S.C. Crook]

A few of the survivors of the Class 'D34' 4-4-0s worked out their final days from Hawick shed. One was No.62471 *Glen Falloch*, seen here passing a well-preserved North British signal as it approaches Canal Junction with the 6.13 p.m. Carlisle-Hawick in September 1959.

[S.C. Crook]

'J36' 0-6-0 No.65312 ambles past the imposing signal box at Canal Junction on 16 July 1962. The tracks in the foreground formed the Silloth branch, and the entrance to the motive power depot is to the left of the locomotive.   [W.S. Sellar]

Canal shed provided the motive power from the Carlisle end of the line and usually housed a varied assortment of locomotives. In the foreground of this view stands 'D31' 4-4-0 No.62281, the last survivor of its class when withdrawn in 1952, which ended its days working on the Silloth branch. Behind the coaling plant are examples of 'K3' 2-6-0 and 'J36' 0-6-0 and to the right 'J39' 0-6-0s with an 'N15/1' 0-6-2T in between; 3 May 1953.   [R.H. Leslie]

With the opening of the marshalling yard at Kingmoor early in 1963, all traffic was concentrated there, and the small local freight yards, including Canal, were closed down. Class 'V2' 2-6-2 No.60846 climbs slowly up to the bridge over the Glasgow line with an Edinburgh-bound freight, which it has drawn tender-first from Kingmoor New Yard along a spur (visible on the right of the photograph), thence ran round the train to begin its journey proper. Passing underneath is rebuilt 'Royal Scot' No.46136 *The Border Regiment*; 8 June 1963.

[R.H. Leslie]

'A3' Pacific No.60097 *Humorist* heads the 1.28 p.m. Carlisle–Edinburgh over the main Glasgow line at Kingmoor on 28 March 1959. This locomotive was the subject of smoke-deflector experiments in the 1930s and, in 1937, became the first of the class to receive a double blast pipe and chimney.

[R.H. Leslie]

A smartly turned-out Class 'J39', No. 64899, bustles along near Kingmoor with the 6.32 p.m. train from Langholm to Carlisle on 23 May 1959. [R.H. Leslie]

The 5.30 p.m. freight from Canal yard to Aberdeen (Craiginches) passing Brunthill siding, near Kingmoor, hauled by 'A2' Pacific No.60532 *Blue Peter*. This locomotive, named after the famous racehorse which won both the Derby and 2000 Guineas in 1939, is now privately preserved in working order. [R.H. Leslie]

'A3' Pacific No.60093 *Coronach* heads the 1.28 p.m. Carlisle-Edinburgh train past Parkhouse Halt, built to serve the adjacent RAF Maintenance Unit; 19 April 1958.   [R.H. Leslie]

The 12.28 p.m. stopping train from Hawick to Carlisle passing the long-closed station at Harker on 19 Apri 1958. At the head is ex-works Class 'D49' 4-4-0 No.62734 *Cumberland*, appropriately stationed at Canal she for much of its life until withdrawal from service in 1961.

[R.H. Leslie

'A2' No.60537 *Bachelor's Button,* one of the less fortunate racehorse names bestowed upon the LNER Pacifics, gleams in the evening sunshine as she storms away from Longtown on the last lap to Carlisle with the 2.36 p.m. from Edinburgh on 16 April 1960.   [R.H. Leslie]

'B1' 4-6-0 No.61404 heads the 3.37 p.m. Carlisle-Edinburgh stopping train through the
pleasant countryside approaching Longtown on 14 August 1954.   [R.H. Leslie]

The Gresley 'V2' 2-6-2s with their high power and short wheelbase were ideally suited to the Waverley Route over which they worked long and hard on both passenger and freight trains. No.60971 swings round a curve on the bank of the River Esk north of Longtown with an Edinburgh–Carlisle freight on 8 April 1961.
[R.H. Leslie]

Another type which had a long association with the Waverley Route was the sturdy-looking 'K3' 2-6-0. They were to be found mainly on freight work and No.61911, nicely polished, was photographed near Scotch Dyke heading a Carlisle-Craiginches goods on 23 May 1959.　　　　　　　　　　　　　　　　　　　　　[R.H. Leslie]

Overleaf: One of the regulars on the line, 'A3' Pacific No.60068 *Sir Visto,* which was stationed at Canal shed from 1940 to 1962, heads the 2.36 p.m. Edinburgh-Carlisle away from Longtown on 21 May 1960. No.60068 was the last of the class to be converted to 'A3' from the original 'A1', in December 1948.　　　[R.H. Leslie]

The 12.00 p.m. Edinburgh–
Carlisle train headed by 'A3'
No.60098 *Spion Kop* passes
Scotch Dyke station on
4 April 1959.   [R.H. Leslie]

Class '4MT' 2-6-0 No.43139 came to Canal shed when new in 1951 and worked regularly on the Langholm branch trains. She is illustrated here heading the 6.22 p.m. through train to Carlisle round the curves near Scotch Dyke on 16 July 1956. The 40 sign was a rather exaggerated restriction for enginemen found these curves could be taken comfortably at over 50 m.p.h. [R.H. Leslie]

Former North British Railway 'D30' 4-4-0 No.62435 *Norna* glides sedately along near Scotch Dyke with a Carlisle-Hawick stopping train on 16 July 1956. [R.H. Leslie]

The Gresley 'A3' Pacifics first appeared on the line in 1928 and worked regularly, chiefly on passenger services, for over thirty years. In their later years, before modification, they tended to become rather run down at times and the syncopated three-cylinder exhaust beat was rousing the echoes as very grimy No.60093 *Coronach*, which came to Ganal shed in 1941, stormed north near Scotch Dyke with the 8.50 a.m. St. Pancras-Edinburgh express on 14 August 1954. [R.H. Leslie]

British Railways Standard Class '2MT' 2-6-0 No.78046, one of the types which replaced the ageing North British locomotives at Hawick in the 1950s, gallops downhill towards Riddings Junction with the 12.18 p.m Hawick-Carlisle on 14 October 1961.

[R.H. Leslie

From Riddings Junction, the line climbed up the hillside overlooking the Liddel valley on a continuous curving gradient of 1 in 100. 'A3' Pacific No.60037 *Hyperion*, had been audible from the moment of restarting from Riddings as she pounded up the bank to Penton with a morning Carlisle-Edinburgh train in May 1958.

[R.H. Leslie]

'A3' Pacific No.60079 *Bayardo* climbs away from Riddings Junction with the 1.45 p.m. Carlisle-Edinburgh on 29 August 1959. In the background is the viaduct which carried the Langholm branch across the Liddel Water.

[R.H. Leslie]

'D34' 4-4-0 No.62484 *Glen Lyon* was another of the class which ended its days on local duties at Hawick shed. She is pictured here in beautifully polished condition, drawing away from Penton with the 12.28 p.m. Hawick–Carlisle on 15 April 1961.

[R.H. Leslie]

The performance of the 'A3' Pacifics was rejuvenated by the fitting of double blast pipes and other modifications in the late 1950s. In contrast to No.60037 on page 31, No.60095 *Flamingo* forges almost effortlessly up the bank towards Penton with the down 'Waverley' on 16 April 1960. [R.H. Leslie]

One rather unusual feature of the line was that north of Scotch Dyke, although it ran within close proximity to Scotland it did not actually enter the country until crossing the Kershope Burn at Kershopefoot station, and even as far north as Riccarton Junction was only about three miles from Northumberland! The countryside around the Liddel valley is very pleasant, and completely unspoiled, especially around Penton, where 'A3' No.60041 *Salmon Trout* is arriving with the leisurely 6.42 a.m. Edinburgh–Carlisle on 26 May 1958. [R.H. Leslie]

'A2/1' Pacific No.60507 *Highland Chieftain* swings over the Liddel Water as it approaches Newcastleton and faces the long climb to Whitrope summit with the down 'Waverley' on 14 June 1958. [R.H. Leslie]

'A3' Pacific No.60095 *Flamingo* leaving Newcastleton with the 2.36 p.m. Edinburgh–Carlisle, 14 June 1958. *Flamingo* came to Canal shed as LNER No.2749 in February 1929 and remained at Carlisle for the whole of its working life until withdrawal from service in April 1961, the only 'A3' to be allocated solely to one shed. The relatively short journeys over the Waverley Route resulted in it recording the lowest mileage figure of the class, just over 1,500,000.   [R.H. Leslie]

A light-weight freight for Carlisle headed by a very clean Class 'D49'—No.62729 *Rutlandshire*—hurries down from the hills past Newcastleton on 15 June 1957.

[R.H. Leslie]

The 3.30 p.m. Carlisle–Edinburgh stopping train, hauled by 'B1' 4-6-0 No.61333, seen leaving Newcastleton to begin the climb to Whitrope in June 1958.

[R.H. Leslie]

'A1' Pacific No.60162 *Saint Johnstoun* crossing Hermitage Viaduct and heading into the hills as it climbs away from Newcastleton with a down train for Edinburgh on 15 April 1961. No.60162 was one of several members of the class which perpetuated some of the names formerly carried by the North British 'Atlantics'.

[R.H. Leslie]

A heavy Carlisle-Edinburgh freight battling with the 1 in 75 gradient approaching Riccarton Junction on 31 May 1952. 'K3' 2-6-0 No.61936 is being banked from Newcastleton to Whitrope summit by 'D30' 4-4-0 No.62420 *Dominie Sampson*.

[J.L. Stevenson]

Some idea of the bleak nature of the country through which the line passed on its way over the Cheviot Hills can be gained from this view of 'A3' No.60037 *Hyperion*, forging up the 1 in 75 gradient at Steele Road with the down 'Waverley' on 16 May 1959.   [R.H. Leslie]

'V2' 2-6-2 No.60819 pauses at lonely Steele Road station with the 3.22 p.m. Carlisle-Edinburgh on 16 May 1959. A few passengers are alighting, some to join the connecting bus service which ran on Saturdays from Bellingham in the North Tyne valley.

[R.H. Leslie]

Arnton Fell dominates the view north from Steele Road station as 'K3' 2-6-0 No.61823
drifts downhill with a freight for Carlisle on 16 May 1959.   [R.H. Leslie]

The veteran former NBR 0-6-0s of Class 'J36' performed much of the banking assistance from both Newcastleton and Hawick. Here, No.65259 gives a sturdy push to a northbound freight near Riccarton Junction on 19 September 1953. [J.L. Stevenson]

Freight trains meeting at the northern end of Riccarton Junction: 'V2' 2-6-2 No.60957 stands with the 11.38 a.m. Carlisle–Millerhill, while the 8.18 a.m. from Millerhill, running late, is headed by 'A1' 4-6-2 No.60118 *Archibald Sturrock*. The fireman of the latter has alighted and is sprinting towards the station; 16 July 1963.

[W.S. Sèllar]

Riccarton Junction was one of the remotest outposts on the whole railway system. The small community depended entirely on the railway, there being no road within miles. The village shop can be seen on the platform as 'D49' 4-4-0 No.62733 *Northumberland* calls with the 12.28 p.m. Hawick–Carlisle on 1 April 1961.

[A. Tyson]

Locomotives were often put in store out in the wilds on a siding alongside the Border Counties line at Riccarton. Former NBR Class 'C15' 4-4-2T No.67459 has the company of former Great Northern Railway Class 'D1' 4-4-0 No.62214—a type which came north in the 1920s and performed much work on branch lines and other light duties—on 19 July 1949.

[J.L. Stevenson]

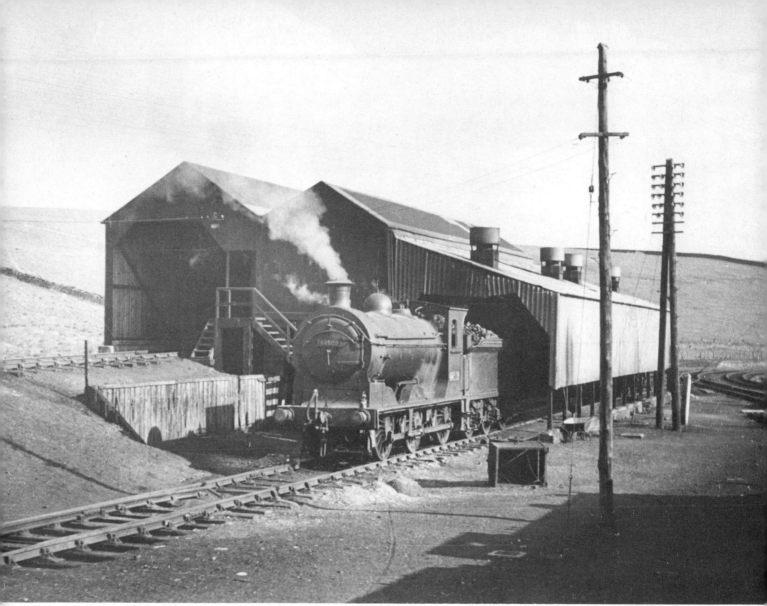

The small engine shed at Riccarton Junction with Class 'J35' 0-6-0 No.64509 resting between banking turns in April 1952; a locomotive from Hawick was usually outshedded here.   [H.C. Casserley]

he Border Counties line left the Waverley Route at Riccarton Junction and wandered off down the North yne Valley to Hexham, through stations with evocative, haunting names like Plashetts, Saughtree and eadwater. A pick-up goods from Hexham, headed by 'J36' 0-6-0 No.65316, arrives at Riccarton on ı May 1952.

[J.L. Stevenson]   **49**

The hard work is over and the fireman relaxes as 'K3' No.61854 begins the long descent to Newcastleton with a south bound freight for Carlisle on 26 May 1956. The train has been banked by a 'J36' 0-6-0 which can be seen standing at Whitrope signal box.

[R.H. Leslie]

'A3' Pacific No.60093 *Coronach* emerges from the deep cutting on the final pull up to Whitrope summit with the 9.00 a.m. St. Pancras-Edinburgh express, which the following year was titled 'The Waverley'. 26 May 1956.

[R.H. Leslie]

Whitrope summit, 1,006′ above sea-level in the Cheviot Hills, with 'A3' Pacific No.60057 *Ormonde* passi
the lonely signal box with the 2.33 p.m. Edinburgh-Carlisle on 26 May 1956.   [R.H. Lesl

'V2' No.60958 slowly climbs the 1 in 96 gradient out of the 1,208 yards-long Whitrope Tunnel and
approaches the summit with an Edinburgh-Carlisle freight on 15 April 1961.   [R.H. Leslie]

The Class 'J38' 0-6-0s were an LNER design of 1926 for heavy freight work in Scotland. They were rare visitors to the southern end of the Waverley Route but on the evening of 15 April 1961 No.65915 was caught heading a light-weight goods for Carlisle past Whitrope summit. [R.H. Leslie]

A view from the brakevan of the 8.18 a.m. Millerhill-Carlisle freight, a capacity load hauled by 'A1' Pacific No.60118 *Archibald Sturrock,* as it climbs the 1 in 75 gradient over the bleak moors towards the northern entrance to Whitrope Tunnel. Leap Hill is prominent on the skyline; 14 August 1963.   [W.S. Sellar]

The 12.28 p.m. Saturday train from Hawick to Carlisle, headed by 'D34' 4-4-0 No.62488 *Glen Aladale,* climbs the 1 in 75 gradient away from Shankend in August 1960.

[S.C. Crook]

The lilting three-cylinder exhaust beat of 'V2' No.60969 echoes around the hills as she pounds up the 1 in 80 towards Stobs on the climb from Hawick to Whitrope with a freight for Carlisle in April 1961.

[R.H. Leslie]

'A3' Pacific No.60079 *Bayardo* restarting the 12.00 p.m. Edinburgh–Carlisle up the 1 in 75 gradient out of the sharply-curved station at Hawick on 1 April 1958. The combination of gradient and curve made starting difficult and it was common practice for most southbound trains to be given a push out of the platform by the station pilot.

[W.S. Sellar]

The 3.22 p.m. Carlisle–Edinburgh train headed by 'A1' No.60159 *Bonnie Dundee* eases carefully around the severe curves as it crosses the Slitrig Water and approaches Hawick on 2 September 1960.

[W.A.C. Smith]

The locomotive shed at Hawick was situated alongside the station at a slightly lower level. Until the early 1960s, there was usually a good selection of former North British engines on view as in this scene on 31 May 1952 which includes 'J36' 0-6-0 No.65232, 'C15' 4-4-2T No.67477 and 'D30' 4-4-0 No.62423 *Dugal Dalgetty*. [J.L. Stevenson]

In the Autumn of 1961, a few of the 'Britannia' Pacifics made redundant on the Western Region were transferred to Canal shed for a while and worked on both passenger and freight trains. One of these, No.70018 *Flying Dutchman*, pulls out of Hawick, past the lofty signal box, with the down 'Waverley' on 7 May 1962. [A.R. Butcher]

'A3' Pacific No.60035 *Windsor Lad*, heading the 6.40 a.m. Edinburgh–Carlisle, takes water at St. Boswells on 22 July 1961. Note the two shunting signals in the foreground, the NB design incorporating a semaphore on a short lattice post alongside a modern disc pattern. [R. Montgomery]

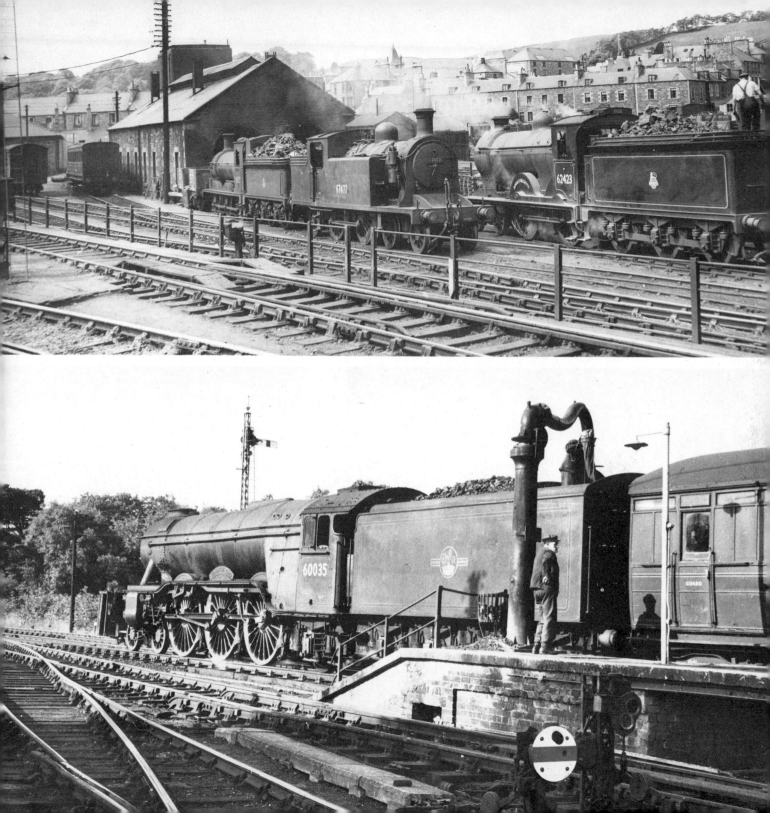

St. Boswells was the junction for the branch line which meandered across the Border country through Kelso to Tweedmouth. These two photographs show typical trains awaiting departure from St. Boswells, the upper one rather appropriately headed by 'D30' 4-4-0 No.62440 *Wandering Willie* on 31 May 1952, and the lower one with 'C15' 4-4-2T No.7472 on 15 May 1948.

[J.L. Stevenson]

A local freight from Hawick to Galashiels headed by 'D30' 4-4-0 No.62421 *Laird O' Monkbarns* passes Melrose on 16 May 1958. One of the footplatemen appears to be reviving the practice of earlier days by going out along the running plate to lubricate the locomotive while on the move, or possibly to investigate trouble!

[W.S. Sellar]

The Waverley Route was frequently affected by snow blockages in Winter, especially on exposed stretches of the line. In this scene 'J36' 0-6-0 No.65327 shows evidence of recent snow clearing activities as it takes a rest at Galashiels on 8 February 1958.

[W.S. Sellar]

nother ageing 'D30', No.62428 *The Talisman*, drawing away from Melrose with the
.11 a.m. (Saturdays-only) stopping train from Hawick to Edinburgh on 17 May 1958.

[W.S. Sellar]

The 'D32' Class 4-4-0s were a Reid design of 1906 for mixed traffic work and operated over much of the North British system. They spent their declining years in the Edinburgh area, although two were stationed at Blaydon for working over the Border Counties line. No.2454, in very clean condition but with a burned smokebox door, is pictured taking water at Galashiels on 15 May 1948. She was withdrawn from service the following September.　　[J.L. Stevenson]

'B1' 4-6-0 No.61345, in very clean condition, begins the long climb to Falahill as it leav
Galashiels with a short Hawick–Millerhill freight on 18 August 1962.　[Douglas Hum

'V2' 2-6-2 No.60813, the only member of the class fitted with a stove-pipe chimney and smoke deflector, heads a Millerhill-Carlisle freight through Galashiels on 30 April 1964.
[A.T. Bramhall]

The Peebles branch diverged from the Waverley Route at Kilnknowe Junction, one mile north of Galashiels, and encountered severe gradients as it wended its way between the Moorfoot and Pentland hills before rejoining the main line at Hardengreen Junction. Class 'V1' 2-6-2T No.67608 awaits departure from Galashiels with the 10.16 a.m. to Edinburgh via Peebles on 13 June 1953.   [J.L. Stevenson]

A very grimy Class 'D34' 4-4-0, No.62490 *Glen Fintaig,* awaits departure from rain-swep
Galashiels with a train to Edinburgh via Peebles on 14 July 1953.   [P.H. Wells

At Fountainhall, the branch to Lauder left the main line. Because of severe weight restrictions, the locomotive which hauled the freight-only service over it was normally a former Great Eastern Railway Class 'J67/1' 0-6-0T, which ran with empty side tanks and was coupled to a tender which contained its water supply. In this form No.68492 is pictured at Galashiels in April 1952.

[H.C. Casserley]

The climb to Falahill is much less severe from the south, the line following the very scenic valley of the Gala Water which is crossed many times in the course of the fifteen miles from Galashiels. Class 'B1' 4-6-0 No.61389 heads a Hawick-Edinburgh train near Stow on 3 June 1965.   [Derek Cross]

'B1' No.61345 tops Falahill summit, 880′ above sea-level in the Moorfoot Hills, 18 miles from Edinburgh, with an Edinburgh-Hawick stopping train on 29 September 1962.   [Douglas Hume]

After the closure of Canal shed in 1963, Kingmoor became responsible for providing motive power from the Carlisle end of the line. As a result, London Midland Region locomotives, especially Stanier Class 5 4-6-0s, appeared in increasing numbers on freights. One of these, No.45082, heads a Carlisle–Edinburgh goods near Fountainhall in May 1965.

[Derek Cross]

The lengthy and heavy car-trains which used the Waverley Route in the 1960s were invariably double-headed, with all manner of unusual combinations of locomotives appearing. On this occasion, 'A3' Pacific No.60087 *Blenheim*, is coupled ahead of Class '4MT' 2-6-0 No.43011 as they battle with a strong wind as well as the 1 in 70 gradient near Falahill on 18 May 1963.

[R. Montgomery]

...other 'Black Five', No.45254, toils up the 1 in 70 gradient on the last stage of the climb ...ween Tynehead and Falahill, heading a Millerhill-Carlisle freight in May 1965.

[Derek Cross]

'V2' 2-6-2 No.60816 storming up the 1 in 70 climb through Fushiebridge with the 2.36 p.m. Edinburgh-Carlisle on 23 May 1959. Note the large bird flying straight through the smoke! [W.S. Sellar]

n Edinburgh-Carlisle freight on the severely curved stretch of line between Fushiebridge and Borthwick nk. 'Britannia' Pacific No.70020 *Mercury* does not appear to be in the best of condition as it toils up the n 70 towards Falahill on 8 May 1963. [W.S. Sellar]

'V3' 2-6-2T No.67624 pulls out of Gorebridge with the 1.02 p.m. stopping train to Edinburgh on 22 May 1959. [W.S. Sellar]

78

The following day, the 1.02 p.m. Gorebridge-Edinburgh is headed by Class 'D49' 4-4-0 No.62715 *Roxburghshire*. This train, a return duty from Waverley, was worked by Dunbar enginemen. 23 May 1959. [W.S. Sellar]

'J37' 0-6-0 No.64556 keeps a tight hold of a coal train from Fushiebridge as it descends the 1 in 70 gradient and prepares to enter the sidings at Lady Victoria Pit in June 1964.   [Derek Cross]

Beyond Fushiebridge the line enters the Lothian industrial area; Class 'A1' 4-6-2 No.60152 *Holyrood*, climbs past Lady Victoria Pit with a Millerhill–Carlisle freight on 5 September 1963.   [Derek Cross]

An impressive view of 'K3' 2-6-0 No.61858 approaching Gorebridge with the 2.50 p.m. Niddrie–Carlisle freight on 9 May 1959.

[W.S. Sellar]

The engine crews of the Hardengreen bankers were sometimes accused of merely 'going for the ride', but 'J36' No.65224 *Mons* produces evidence to the contrary as she blasts away at the rear of the train illustrated opposite, pushing hard up to Falahill. No.65224 was one of the members of the class sent to France for service with the Railway Operating Department during the 1914-18 war. [W.S. Sellar]

'J35' 0-6-0 No.64479, fitted with a tender cab, at Glenesk Junction with a freight train off the Dalkeith branch bound for Hardengreen yard, 21 April 1960.

[W.S. Sellar]

Another 'J37' 0-6-0, No.64561, taking water at Hardengreen Junction during a pause in shunting duties on 27 May 1961. Below; an unusual and rather sad sight on the Waverley Route. London Midland Region rebuilt 'Patriot' Class No.45535 *Sir Herbert Walker, KCB,* formerly used on express passenger turns from Edge Hill (Liverpool) shed, is demoted to hauling a Millerhill-Carlisle freight at Hardengreen on 25 May 1963.

[R. Montgomery]

'A3' Pacific No.60079 *Bayardo*, heads an Edinburgh-Carlisle train at Millerhill in August 1958 and is passing the site of the large marshalling yard on which construction had recently commenced. [Derek Cross]

The same location five years later, changed almost out of recognition, with Millerhill yard in operation. 'B1' 4-6-0 No.61354 is passing through the lines of wagons with an Edinburgh–Hawick train on 5 September 1963.

[Derek Cross]

Overleaf: Lothian Bridge carries the line over the River South Esk near Newtongrange. The train is the 5.11 p.m. Edinburgh–Galashiels headed by 'B1' 4-6-0 No.61341 on 24 May 1962.　　　[W.A.C. Smith]

Standard 'Britannia' Pacific No.70020 *Mercury* draws out of Millerhill yard with the 3.25 p.m. freight to Carlisle on 8 May 1963. A Class 'J38' 0-6-0 is on the up main line with another freight.   [W.S. Sellar]

The Waverley Route diverges from the East Coast main line at Portobello East Junction and immediately begins a sharp climb at 1 in 80 to Niddrie South Junction. 'A2/3' Pacific No.60519 *Honeyway* storms up the bank past Niddrie North Junction with the 2.36 p.m. Edinburgh-Carlisle on 17 October 1955. No.60519 was one of three members of Class 'A2/3' to retain the plain double chimney to the end of their lives.

[W.S. Sellar]

The largest locomotives to work over the Waverley Route in North British Railway days were the celebrated 'Atlantics' designed by W.P. Reid in 1906 which handled the heaviest trains until gradually superseded by the new LNER Class 'A3' Pacifics from 1929 onwards. They were imposing, sturdy machines with a healthy appetite for coal and a voice to match, and carried splendid Scottish names, some of which were associated with the Waverley Route. No.9904 *Holyrood*, in early LNER livery, which must have made the Edinburgh–Carlisle journey countless times, stands in Craigentinny sidings, west of Portobello, in 1925.

[R.D. Stephen]

The motive power depot at St. Margaret's, situated alongside the East Coast main line between Portobello and Waverley station, provided many of the locomotives for freight trains over the Waverley Route as well as for secondary services in the Edinburgh area. This view, taken on a murky day, depicts a variety of locomotives including 'K3', 'Black Five', 'J35' and 'D34' 4-4-0 No.62488 *Glen Aladale* which seven years later ended its life working on the Waverley Route from Hawick; 16 July 1953.

[P.H. Wells]

'V2' 2-6-2 No.3665, in war-time black livery and carrying its original number, passing Portobello station with the 12.10 p.m. Edinburgh–Carlisle in February 1946. [J.L. Stevenson]

94

One of the familiar Class 'A3' Pacifics, No.37 *Hyperion*, in LNER livery, backs on to the 2.35 p.m. to Carlisle at Waverley station on 15 May 1948.   [J.L. Stevenson]

Tank engines at the east end of Waverley station on 15 May 1948.   Above; one of the graceful former North British Railway Class 'C16' 4-4-2s, No.7492, glides towards the station with a local train.   Below; 'V3' 2-6-2 No.7605, still carrying the abbreviated war-time 'NE' letters on its side tanks, reverses out of the station after bringing in a stopping train from Galashiels.   [J.L. Stevenson]

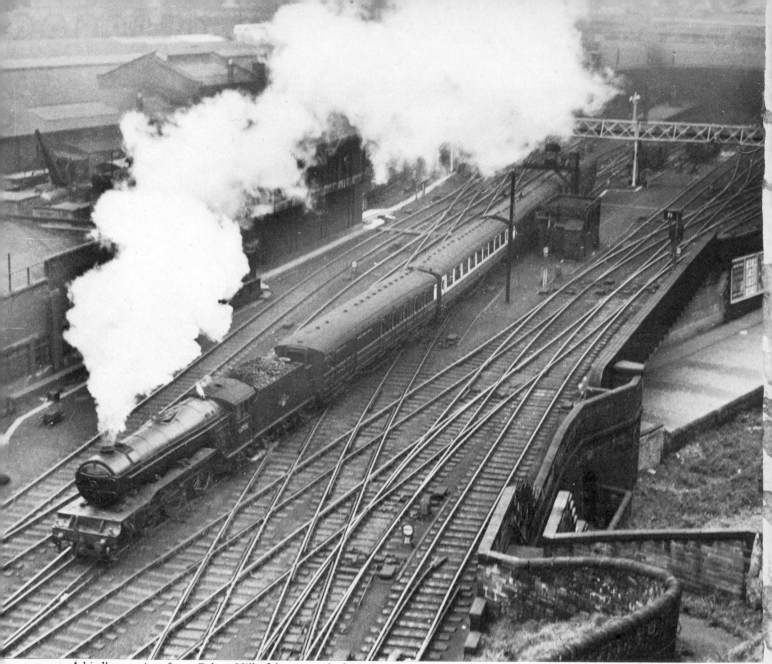

A bird's-eye view from Calton Hill of the east end of Waverley station. 'V2' 2-6-2 No.60951 is departing with the lightly-loaded 12.05 p.m. to Carlisle on 27 October 1958.

[G.H. Robin]